THE PROPER WAY OF INTERACTING WITH THE POLICE

Tyrone Baugh

THE PROPER WAY OF
INTERACTING WITH THE POLICE

<u>Acknowledgements</u>

Special thanks to my beautiful wife, Mahadiah Muhammad (*See her website at* www.mysisterbond.com); my sons, Jalil Muhammad, Joshua Muhammad and Malichi Muhammad; and my one and only daughter, Jaiyana Muhammad.

Thanks also to Niya Muhammad (computergurl.com) for designing the front and back covers.

<u>Introduction</u>

The motivation to write this book came about from seeing so many Black, Brown, Indigenous and poor Whites losing their lives at the hands of law enforcement.

Just in the province of Ontario, Canada, Black and Middle Eastern drivers are still being stopped at disproportionately high rates, according to *CBC News Data*. Also, based on reports by *CTV News*, an indigenous person in Canada is more than 10 times more likely to have been shot and killed by a police officer than a white person since 2017.

In the United States, a black person is

allegedly killed every 24 hours in by law enforcement. According to the *Washington Post*, the rate at which black Americans are killed by police is more than twice as high as the rate for white Americans.

The Police is responsible for his or her own actions. I am responsible for my own behaviour at all times. You can only control your own behaviour. This book will give you the necessary tools to assist you when dealing with a police encounter.

You will learn the *do's* and *don'ts* when interacting with the Police. This will hopefully minimize your risk of getting injured, going to jail or ending up dead.

I am a Religious Person

Whether you say God, Jesus, Allah, Buddha, Jah, Yahweh, Mother Nature, Great Mother or Father, everything that is in existence wants to live. It is incumbent upon you and me to protect and preserve our lives at all cost.

I don't want you in a coffin.

On the side of the road is not the place to adjudicate your case.

My job is to get you home alive.

Definition of "Proper" (Adjective)

- Genuine, Suitable or Appropriate; Correct, Right, Respectable, Accepted.

- Please note that this is not the <u>ONLY</u> way to deal with the Police.

This book is not anti-police or anti-law enforcement.

#Anti-Police (**No!**)

#Hate the Pigs, DeathToThePolice etc. (**No!**)

Once we have motion, we <u>MUST</u> have

<u>LAWS</u>, rules, and people to regulate those laws.

Without laws, we would live in a world of chaos. We need laws that are just, and laws that are applied equally to all, regardless of creed, class, gender or colour in a civilized society.

Why have respect for **<u>AUTHORITY</u>?** They have the Power, the Command, and they also have the upper hand and the dominant position. They can literally take your life.

Our Perception *vs* Our Reality When Interacting with the Police, and What the Police See

➢ Make and model of my vehicle; Colour of my vehicle; License plate, Number of people inside the vehicle

➢ The owner of the vehicle; The vehicle; Registered or Unregistered/records of the Vehicle; Gender and/or RACE of the persons or people inside the Vehicle) etc.

<u>Our Perception of the Police</u>

Many people think the police view them as follows:

➢ I am a PHD student

- ➢ I am an honour student

- ➢ I'm in the church choir/a community activist

- ➢ I love the Police, (fear) loving father and business owner (RACE), I attend the mosque/church on a regular basis.

Some Things to Remember When Interacting with the Police

- Make sure your hands are always visible.

- Be respectful.

- Be calm.

- Never be the aggressor.

- Don't make any sudden movements.

- Never call him/her outside of their names.

- Keep your hands to yourself.

- Obey the officer's command.

- <u>Comply with the *officer's* terms/not *yours.*</u>

Dealing with a Roadside Stop

- Have all your documents ready.

- If it is night, make sure your lights are on.

- Proper attitude will determine your altitude.

- Wind down your windows (if possible).

- Let the officer know exactly what you are going to do next.

- Try to pull over in an area that is safe for you and the officer.

- Keep your car clean, to avoid suspicion.

Which Person Are You?

- Riding dirty (drugs) cannot help you!

- "All Police are Pigs (Fire on Babylon)"

- "I know my rights"

- "I don't have to show you my I.D."

- "My cousin, uncle, dad, brother, mom, neighbour, third aunt is an officer."

- "It is because I'm BLACK (so-called visible minority)!!!!"

- "That could never be me..."

- "I am just going to crack my window"

- "I am in Police College"

Compliance *vs* Compliance on My Terms

Remember when Mom or Dad said wash the dishes, but we wanted to wash them on our terms?

- I am just going to crack my window, And slide my documents to the officer when I'm ready.

- I am in the passenger seat so I will just do my own thing.

- I will just show you my documents, but you cannot take them.

*You **<u>MUST</u>** comply with the officer on his or her terms.*

<u>NEVER</u> take on the "shoot me and see" approach. You might be right, and the officer might be completely in the wrong; however, you may still end up crippled, or dead.

At the Root

For you to have an inkling of what or who you are dealing with, you must know some history of how policing actually came into being.

The purpose for it coming into being was as a result of the mindset of those who were in power. This had set things into motion.

If a system had been built on catching runaway slaves, then one must conclude that there will always be some remnant of that still lingering on; and it will eventually rear its ugly head.

If you cannot fathom the depth of a thing,

you are not equipped to deal with it!

I am not implying that ALL officers fall under this banner, but I would be remiss in my duties to ignore the origins of such a system.

Can We Reform the System?

You will have to answer this question yourself.

This is the debate we see on all these TV shows and in various town hall meetings for decades, and to no avail.

Ask yourself; what will happen if you just keep sweeping away the cobwebs?

What would the spider do? Will you ever get tired of sweeping?

Please write down your answer!

Thermostat *vs* Thermometer Approach

One of these devices will check the temperature in the household, and one helps to regulate the temperature.

We must be able to know which device to use, when dealing with the police. If you notice, the officer may be trying to bait or trap you into losing your cool.

You must be able to rise above your emotions and change the direction of the discussion by using the **Thermostat approach:**

- Obey those in authority, unless it conflicts

with your religion or way of life.

- Don't give the officer any reason to exert force from his or her authority.

- Show respect! Do unto others as you would like to be done unto you.

- At the end of the day, <u>ALL of US</u> want to make it home safely.

- <u>The side of the road is not a place to adjudicate your case!</u>

Actual Threat *vs* Perceived Threat

Being a police officer is extremely difficult, stressful, and a very hard job. But this does not give them the right to say, "I feared for my life," based only on what they *perceived* as a threat. This may lead to the officer taking someone else's life.

The police may have to make a split-second decisions. The officer is now in a high-risk position that will determine what he or she perceives to be life-threatening.

The police and I want to make it home

to our families. But the Police doesn't have the right to be judge, funeral director, the Grim Reaper and the undertaker.

Most officers share this statement, whether they will admit it or not. (I, personally, would rather be judged by 12 than carried by 6. Don't give them the chance to be judge!)

How many officers are required to inspect or detain one individual? The Lion VS the Hyenas.

The hyena knows that he cannot take on a young male lion by himself. The hyena (system) is natural enemy to the lion (you). It was constructed like that!

After hundreds of years under oppression and tyranny, The Original Lion has become a trained circus lion generations later. The lion has become entertainment for both the trainer and the audience.

Being a good feline, the trainer knows that this is a 400-pound lion (You), and if the lion (you) ever become awake, off goes his/her limbs.

When a system has a people under oppression for this long, deep down inside they know innately that this will not last. So, they have systems in place to ensure they will continue to rule.

When dealing with the Police, you **MUST** ensure you do all you can so that they do not "fear for their lives".

Reading this book does not guarantee that you will not be harassed, arrested, called out of your name, or even be shot by the police.

In applying these methods, hopefully it will minimize the chances of a negative outcome when interacting with the police.

My job is to get you home alive.

~.~

Remember, the objective is to make it home alive.

Yes, even if you think that makes you a punk.

About the Author

Graduating with a diploma in Police Foundation, Tyrone Baugh worked with the police for several years as a liaison between the police and youths.